Through My Eyes

About the Author

Growing up, Jessica Parker always struggled to communicate how she was feeling and thinking. She never understood why she felt so different from everyone else. Then, in November 2023, Jessica was diagnosed with autism at the age of sixteen. Her first poem, *My Autism Poem*, was written when her family were at work and school. Later that day, when she showed it to them, they were amazed, not knowing it would lead to many more. She has learnt that writing poems is an amazing tool for her to communicate her exact thoughts and feelings. They also help others to understand her.

Jessica Parker
___

Through My Eyes

Vanguard Press

VANGUARD PAPERBACK

© Copyright 2025
Jessica Parker

The right of Jessica Parker to be identified as author of
this work has been asserted by her in accordance with the
Copyright, Designs and Patents Act 1988.

All Rights Reserved

No reproduction, copy or transmission of this publication
may be made without written permission.
No paragraph of this publication may be reproduced,
copied or transmitted save with the written permission of the publisher, or in
accordance with the provisions
of the Copyright Act 1956 (as amended).

Any person who commits any unauthorised act in relation to this publication
may be liable to criminal prosecution and civil claims for damages.

A CIP catalogue record for this title is available from the British Library.

ISBN 978-1-83794-949-6

This is a work of fiction. Names, characters, businesses, places, events and
incidents are either the products of the author's imagination or used in a
fictitious manner. Any resemblance to actual persons, living or dead, or actual
events is purely coincidental.

*Vanguard Press is an imprint of
Pegasus Elliot Mackenzie Publishers Ltd.*
www.pegasuspublishers.com

First Published in 2025

**Vanguard Press
Sheraton House Castle Park
Cambridge England**

Printed & Bound in Great Britain

Dedication

For my family because of all the love and support they give me. But most of all, for believing in me.

Acknowledgements

Thank you so much to my family for supporting and believing in me through all the ups and downs of life, especially for fighting the battle when I'm struggling too. Thank you to Dani, Ian and Sinead at CAMHS for their ongoing support for me and my family. Thank you to The Pilgrim School for always brightening my day and making me smile, especially Mel, Lisa, Chantel and Sam.

Contents

My Autism Poem: 13
I Try to Communicate: 15
How I Feel When Lessons Start: 16
I Wish I Had Friends: 17
My Parents: 19
Different: 20
Chad: 22
Behind on Assignments: 24
Gus: 25
Rex: 26
The Forever Home, I Wish You Weren't In: 27
It Makes Me Happy: 29
Happy and Proud: 30
Lead-up to Christmas: 31
My College Work: 32
Sensory Overload Exhaustion: 33
My Diagnosis: 34
Always Feeling Lonely: 35
I Always Stay the Same: 36
I Want to Go a Day Without Feeling Like This: 37
I Want It to Change: 39
I Hope Sooner Rather Than Later: 40
What Naomi Has Given Me: 41
What Naomi Has Taken from Me: 42
I'm So Excited to Go Home: 43
I Don't Know What to Do: 44

I've Struggled Being Back Home: 45
I Want To: 46
It's Naomi, Not Me: 47
Why Did Naomi Choose Me? 48
To Future Me: 49
Thank You for That Family Call: 51
Thank You to My Past Self: 52
Why Won't She Go Away: 53
Horrible Memories from the Place I Hate Most: ... 55
I'll be Forever Grateful: 58
Hidden Strength: 59

My Autism Poem:

I wish I was normal,
Like everyone else,
But my brain works differently,
Like nobody else.

Some textures feel strange,
And bug my brain.
Sudden loud noises
Can cause my ears pain.
Movement from crowds
Can tug my head around.
My head can't cope –
Sensory overload.

I study,
I mimic,
Groups of people,
To be like them –
The other people.

No matter how honest,
How kind,
How much I try,
I just get judged,
Ignored,
No reply.

I don't like change,
I need a routine:
Goodnight,
Love you,
See you tomorrow
Are always my last words
Before I go to sleep.

Yet I'm told I'm normal,
Just like everyone else.
I wish I could see
What others see in myself.

I Try to Communicate:

I try to communicate,
Say how I feel,
But sometimes,
My mouth feels sealed.

My brain won't let me
Say my emotions.
I feel trapped and lonely,
So I keep to myself
How I feel.

If my brain lets me say,
Express how I feel,
My mouth suddenly
Becomes unsealed.
My emotions slowly reveal
How I truly feel.

How I Feel When Lessons Start:

I sit there,
Twisting my pen,
Tapping my leg,
Anxiously waiting,
For noise to fill my head.

They all sit down,
In groups,
Big and loud –
The scratching of chairs
And bags being thrown down.

They pull out their paper,
Laptops and pens,
Waiting for the lesson to start.
Yet I'm waiting for it to end.

I Wish I Had Friends:

I wish I weren't myself.
I wish I were like everyone else –
Everyone who has friends,
Who are never alone
And never by themselves.

The one friend I had
Often avoids me now.
It's always the same –
Cancelling at the last minute,
Saying sorry,
But does she really mean it?

It's always the same words:
I'm busy,
Too much work,
My room's messy.

But I always agree
And say, "It's fine,
Maybe another time."
But deep down,
It hurts inside.

People avoid me,
Try to ignore me.
But this person didn't –

Until now.
Everyone my age
Avoids me.

My Parents:

They never judge me
Or try to ignore me.
But most of all,
They never avoid me.

I always feel heard,
Never misunderstood.
I can be my true self,
Without pretending
To be anybody else.

They understand
That I need a routine,
That I struggle with my senses,
That expressing how I feel
Doesn't always come naturally.

When I do struggle
And say that I'm fine,
They recognise
I might be telling
A little white lie.

But when I'm around them,
I don't have to hide,
Even though
I might do it sometimes.

Different:

People don't know
How it feels
To have been alone
For sixteen years.

They have friends,
People around them,
People to talk to,
Whereas I don't.
I never have,
And I don't think
I ever will.

I always feel alone,
With no messages on my phone,
Nothing to wake up to,
And no one like me,
Or my age,
To talk to.

I try my best,
But it's never good enough.
Sooner than later,
They'll pretend
I wasn't there.

I thought I had friends,

But I didn't really.
They used me
And bullied me,
Then they ignored me.

I wish I had friends,
Like most people my age.
I wish people would
Treat me the same.

But in the end,
I don't understand
Why I'm not treated the same
By people my own age.

Chad:

I wish you were here,
Greeting me at the door,
With a wagging tail
And happy paws.

I miss the feeling of you,
Curled up by my feet,
Sat under the table
When we would eat.

I miss hearing your bark,
Your scratch at the door,
The sound your paws made
As you walked,
And the sound your bed made
On the floor.

I miss feeding you
And playing tug of war,
And when you would
Lean on me,
Especially after a long walk.

But most of all,
I miss your version
Of a human hug –
The Chaddie cuddle.

I wish you were here,
Instead of being there.
I wish I could see you.
Life is just not fair.

Behind on Assignments:

The constant fear
Of being behind,
Buried with
Endless assignments
And lessons online.

I have loads to do
That will soon be overdue,
With daily emails
Telling me
What I need to do.

I want to catch up,
Though it looks too much.
But the longer I leave it,
More assignments
Will build up.

Gus:

I love the way,
When I see you,
Without control,
Your body wiggles,
Never failing
To make me giggle.

I love the way
You must find
Your favourite
Comfort toy
Before going outside.

I love the way
You nudge your nose
Against my leg,
Waiting for me
To pet your head.

I love the way
You want to stay
Inside your crate,
Not going outside
Before your bedtime.

Rex:

I love the way
You curl on my lap
And snuggle around
My dressing gown.

I love the way
You're so sneaky,
Using puppy dog eyes
When you get tired
And sleepy.

I love the way
You give cuddles,
Leaning on me
As you snuggle.

I love the way
You mess around,
When you get so excited,
You can't stay on the ground.

The Forever Home, I Wish You Weren't In:

I had to watch you
Slowly fade away,
Losing control
Without having a say.

Not seeing clearly,
You slowly lost your sight,
Staring into the fire
Almost every night.

Not coming every time
When you were called,
We eventually realised
You needed a loud voice.

The day you died
Was the worst day of my life.
The images keep replaying
Every day in my mind.

I remember your eyes
Widening with fright.
I think you knew
What they were going to do.

As the muzzle
Was placed on you,
We went into the other room,
Shaking and crying,
As I could hear
What was happening.

When I went back,
I remember seeing you,
Sleeping but not really –
You weren't moving.

We said our goodbyes
Before they carried you out,
Wrapped in our blankets,
You were placed in their van.

They drove away,
Taking you with them.
We got you back,
But you were in
Your new forever home.

It Makes Me Happy:

Unlike most people,
I like the rain.
It makes me happy
As it falls to the ground
Around me.

I love hearing the noise
Against my hood,
And when I'm outside,
It taps on the shed roof.

When I wake up
And hear the overflow pipe,
I know it's been raining
Through the night.

People think I'm weird
When I stand in the rain,
But I like the way it feels
On my hair
And on my face.

Happy and Proud:

I sat down one evening
And wrote my feelings,
Not realising the difference
These poems could make.

The day I got told
My work could be used
By helping people
Who may struggle
The same way I do.

I felt happy and proud
Of what I've achieved,
With the hope of helping others
Who may be in need.

I hope it helps
The people like me,
And even the people
Who view the world
A little differently.

Lead-up to Christmas:

My favourite time of year
Will soon be here,
When the songs start to play,
And the tree will soon be made.

I'll soon be wrapping presents
That no one knows about,
Hoping for smiley faces
When the big day comes around.

The opening of calendars,
One door at a time,
Until the night before
The big day arrives.

My College Work:

Slowly working through it,
One day at a time,
Getting things done
That's been on my mind.

Feeling happy, I'm achieving
A little bit at a time,
Which will get bigger
As time goes by.

Thank you for reassuring me
That I'm doing just fine,
Even though I say I don't –
I need that sometimes.

Sensory Overload Exhaustion:

I started my shift
Doing all right.
I took my medication,
Doing one task at a time.

Things started getting worse
As the crowds piled in:
First the bright lights,
Loud noises –
Worse when more people came in.

My heart started to race
As all the loud noises
Rattled through my head.
I couldn't stop or think.

I got told to have a break,
Hoping to get away
From the loudness filling my head.
But instead, I cried
And broke down inside.

Completely exhausted,
They took me home,
Away from all the noise –
But not on my own.

My Diagnosis:

I knew I had autism,
Though I was hoping I didn't.
The day I got diagnosed,
The world felt a little different.

It all made sense –
The way I behave.
It all fell into place,
Though I didn't know
What to do or say.

I thought it was bad,
But it really isn't.
I thought I was abnormal,
Though I'm just different.

I finally have an answer
To why I'm this way.
They even say autistic people
Have a more complicated brain.

Always Feeling Lonely:

I always feel lonely,
Day in, day out.
Sometimes I cry
Because I'm missing out.

I often see photos
And videos on my phone,
Of people having fun,
But I'm always on my own.

I would love to have friends
And have fun in my younger years,
But as time goes on,
I seem nothing like my peers.

They're having fun,
Not wasting a day,
But I'm on my own –
Tomorrow will be the same.

I Always Stay the Same:

People say I'm thin
And that I look great,
But I really hate my body
In almost every way.

I hate my waistline,
Worse when I sit down,
And my big thighs
That jiggle around.

I hate my arms,
Especially in summer,
When it gets hot,
I can't hide them any longer.

I hate it when I wear socks
Or clothing around my waist,
Sometimes leaving red lines –
Maybe I'm overweight.

I wish I was skinnier
And had a better shape.
No matter how hard I try,
I'll never be the right weight.

No matter what I eat
Or how much I train,
It never feels good enough –
I always stay the same.

I Want to Go a Day Without Feeling Like This:

My relationship with food
Isn't good at the minute.
I want to eat that chocolate,
But I can't bring myself to do it.

I just want to eat
Without having a second thought.
My weight's slowly dropping,
Though I'm struggling to eat more.

If I eat unhealthily
Or eat anything really,
Especially if I'm full,
I feel really guilty.

Food is always on my mind,
Though it's really hard to eat.
No matter what I eat or how much,
I get this horrible feeling.

Now used to feeling
Either starving or sick,
But I want to eat anything
Without feeling like this.

If I feel full
Or eat unhealthily,
I feel the need to punish myself
Am I going crazy?

I Want It to Change:

I want to cut myself
Most of the time.
What is going on
Inside my mind?

Whenever I eat,
I want to cry.
I'm trying my best,
Though it takes time.

My stomach is full,
Though so is my plate.
It was never like this –
I want it to change.

I Hope Sooner Rather Than Later:

A lovely lady
Made me realise today,
If I cut my food,
I'll get weaker by the day.

We're planning to bake,
To keep busy as we talk,
With the same struggles as me
And with similar thoughts.

Having someone to talk to
Who feels a similar way –
It might help both of us,
As the feeling likes to stay.

She said it takes time,
But it'll get better.
I'm hoping that it will,
Sooner rather than later.

What Naomi Has Given Me:

She got me admitted
To the place everyone hates.
She made me bed-bound,
With multiple overnight stays.

She made me have a cannula,
That they've had to replace,
With daily IV fluids
Running through my veins.

She made me have blood tests
In the same arm every day,
And blood-thinning injections
Every night that I stay.

She made me have blood sugar tests,
Multiple times a day.
She's given me many hypos
And lift drinks throughout our stay.

She's left me sore and bruised,
With plenty of stomach aches,
Feeling lightheaded
And having to be weighed.

What Naomi Has Taken from Me:

She has taken so much
In a short amount of time.
She's taken away everything
That I love in life.

She's taken away my home
And my family from me.
We can't see them much –
They are so far away from me.

She's taken away my college.
I miss the animals I used to see.
She's taken away my work
And my wages from me.

I wanted to start driving lessons
As soon as I turned seventeen,
But she made that unsafe
And stole that from me.

She took away daily tasks,
Such as walking from me,
And made working out
A dangerous thing for me.

I'm So Excited to Go Home:

We're finally going home,
To the place we love most.
It seems like forever ago
Since we were last at home.

We can be back together
With Dad and Jack at home.
We can finally see the dogs –
I wonder how happy they'll go!

We get to sleep in our own beds,
Much comfier than these,
And watch our own telly tonight.
Our family will be complete.

We get to see Nan and Grandad,
In our home instead of here.
It'll be nice to see them
In a place we love so dear.

I Don't Know What to Do:

Naomi keeps screaming
That I can't have what I'm craving.
She says it's too high in calories
And far too unhealthy.

Naomi keeps telling me
I definitely can't have both –
I would end up obese.
Why can't she leave me alone?

If I listen to what she tells me,
I keep thinking about what I crave,
But then I end up spiralling
And I think about it all day.

If I don't listen to her
And I have what I crave,
I satisfy my thoughts,
Although she still stays.

Is it the right thing,
Eating exactly what I crave?
Or should I listen to Naomi
And the things she says?

I've Struggled Being Back Home:

I weirdly found it easier
In the place far from here,
With less people to interfere
And less comments for my ears.

I've struggled since being home –
A change in my routine,
As well as what people say
That's often hurtful to me.

I've had more positive days
In the place far from here.
I haven't had a full good day yet
In the place I love so dear.

As much as I love my home
And my whole family with me,
I just want a complete good day.
Will life get easier to ignore Naomi?

I Want To:

I want to go back to college
And see the animals on the unit.
I want to go back to work
And have the wages that come with it.

I want to start driving lessons
Now I'm in the legal age limit.
I just want my life back –
It's not too much to ask for, is it?

I want to go back to the farm
And see those cheeky goats,
And work with my friend Holly,
Chatting as we go.

I want to train again,
Doing the workouts I did before,
Without Naomi in my earhole
Telling me I need to do more.

I want to eat out in cafes,
Like I did before,
Without Naomi saying things,
Giving me second thoughts.

It's Naomi, Not Me:

I'm sorry for what I say –
I never mean it.
I hope you all know
It's Naomi who's doing it.

She gets frustrated,
Knowing you're helping me,
Making me say things
To separate our family.

Every time horrible words
Leave my mouth,
I feel really shocked
And immediately feel bad.

I feel out of control;
The anxiety builds in me.
I feel like I could explode –
I really hate Naomi.

It's hard to understand
Those words aren't from me.
Although you can't see it,
The words are Naomi's.

Why Did Naomi Choose Me?

I always think, why me?
Why not the people who bullied me?
Why can't they suffer
With something like Naomi?

They share something in common –
They've both been horrible to me.
Why can't they be trapped
In the painful claws of Naomi?

Is it horrible of me to say
I want them to suffer and not me?
But is that the bad thing I've done
To deserve the crippling pain of Naomi?

To Future Me:

Although it's hard to see it,
You really need to eat it.
If Naomi tells you no,
The more you should do it.

It gets easier over time,
Although you might not see it.
The blueberry muffin is proof –
It gets easier the more you do it.

As you already know,
Missing just one thing
Makes you feel weaker,
Giving Naomi the path to win.

Naomi will always hurt you
If you listen to her lies.
She hasn't done any good –
She nearly made you die.

She'll twist the words of others,
Causing your mind to spin.
Your family is helping you –
They don't want Naomi to win.

Remember, they're your family,
Not like the evil Naomi within.

They love and support you;
They want you to win.

We've come so far
From Naomi's tight grip.
Although we're still recovering,
It's getting easier to slip.

We've got a long journey ahead,
But each day is a little easier.
She sometimes takes control,
But we are making her weaker.

One day, we'll finally be free
From the claws of Naomi.
She'll forever be in our past,
But not in the future of you and me.

Thank You for That Family Call:

A few hours from the tube,
I was refusing any food.
After a family call from home,
It flipped my point of view.

I can't explain the feeling –
My thinking suddenly flipping.
Going from zero amount of food,
I decided to take a bite or two.

If that call hadn't come through,
I might have had the tube.
So thank you, Mum and Dad –
The timing was on cue.

Thank You to My Past Self:

I'm so pleased you took
That very first bite.
If you hadn't done so,
I don't know where I'd be tonight.

I remember it was difficult –
That battle in your head.
I remember the horrible feeling
And what Naomi said.

Then, it was all dreadful;
Now, it's ups and downs.
Because of what you started,
I'm where I am now.

Why Won't She Go Away:

They say it gets easier
With each day that goes by,
But I'm starting to feel
Like that is a lie.

I've stuck to the plan,
Following what they say,
But Naomi is getting worse
Each day that I stay.

She's louder, and more frequent,
Especially at night.
I fear going to bed;
It's when she wraps tight.

There are more downs than ups –
I'm starting to lose the fight.
I'm having more meltdowns,
And death is on my mind.

I'm starting to think
Naomi is here to stay.
I'm really struggling to cope –
Why won't she go away?

I'm following the plan,
And everything they say,

Naomi makes me draw lines,
Because of the food I've ate.

A slight change in routine
Makes me want to scream.
I'm struggling to adapt –
It's really affecting me.

I wish I could have a day
Where she wasn't in my mind.
Why did she pick me?
She makes me want to die.

Horrible Memories from the Place I Hate Most:

Back in the hospital –
But for Mum this time,
It brings back memories,
I don't want to revive.

The feeling of the lift,
Pushing open heavy doors,
That leads to a place
With a white ceiling and floors.

I felt my anxiety building,
My heart racing as we walked,
Through those long corridors,
Passing all the wards.

The memories of the side room
Came flooding back to me –
Staying at Lincoln Hospital,
And all they did to me.

The bleeping of machinery
That drills through my mind,
Instantly brings back memories
Of all those horrible nights.

The prick of all those needles,
Blood tests and thinners –
So many awful memories
And the pain that comes with it.

The memories of the cannula,
Scratching when I'd move,
I wanted to stay still,
But that's something I couldn't do.

I had lots of ten-hour drips,
The weird feeling of it flowing in,
An awful stinging sensation,
That yellow one would bring.

Seeing a shower room today,
Brought back all those times,
I couldn't wash my hair,
So Mum had to for a while.

The time I passed out,
Came back into my mind,
Remembering how I felt,
I was so scared that night.

Although I still have scars,
And bruises from my stay,
I'm not there any more,
It's all going to be okay.

I kept myself distracted,
In the place I hate most,
But it's all okay now
Because we're back home.

I'll be Forever Grateful:

Although I don't say it,
It means the world to me –
All the support you've given
In my Naomi recovery.

Thank you for changing things
To make it easier for me,
And the sacrifices you've made
To help me feel more free.

Supporting me through meals,
Snacks and hot drinks.
I've had many wobbles,
But you've helped me through this.

Naomi would've taken over
If it wasn't for you both.
I'll be forever grateful –
I can't fight her on my own.

Hidden Strength:

I recently got told,
And it really hit home,
How strong I must be
To change it on my own.

I was heading down a path
That the majority can't control,
But I managed to change it,
And I brought us home.

She was filling out forms
To force a tube down my throat,
To have me stay longer
In the place I hate most.

She went back to work
After taking a day off.
She was shocked being told
That she was able to stop.

She said I must have strength,
Maybe hidden inside,
Because I never realised –
I just knew I had to fight.